Dedicated to:

my mom & dad…who let me paint the walls

my grandmother…my ardent admirer

& last but not least my 5 boys…my true Loves

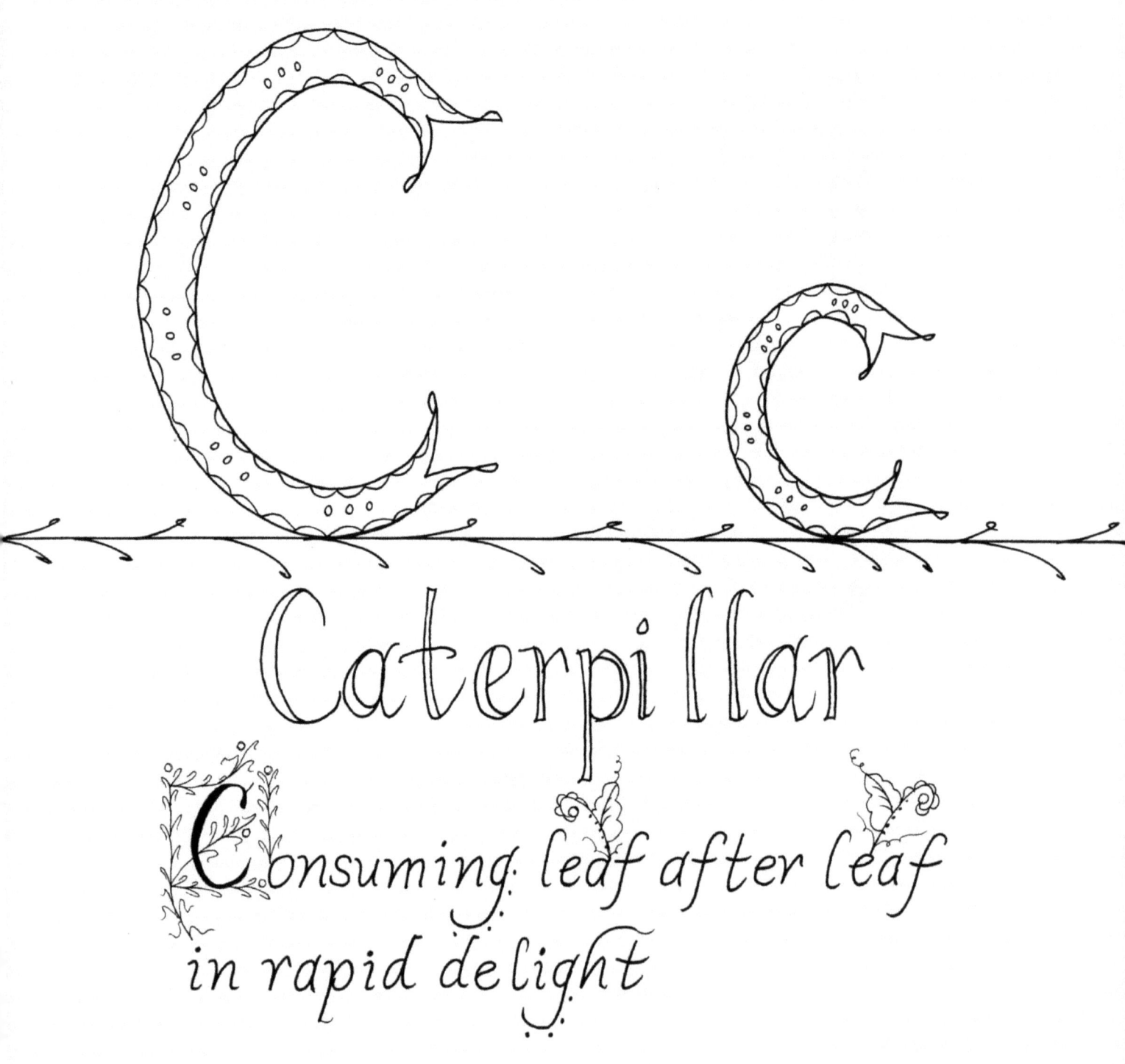

Caterpillar

Consuming leaf after leaf in rapid delight

Inchworm

Arching inches along
a purple passion flower's back

Jackrabbit
Pounding thumps
in the coolness of a starred midnight

Kk Kingfisher

Flashing saber silver scales are gulped in one quick bite

Ll

Lily

Basking unfurled in flames of orangest glory

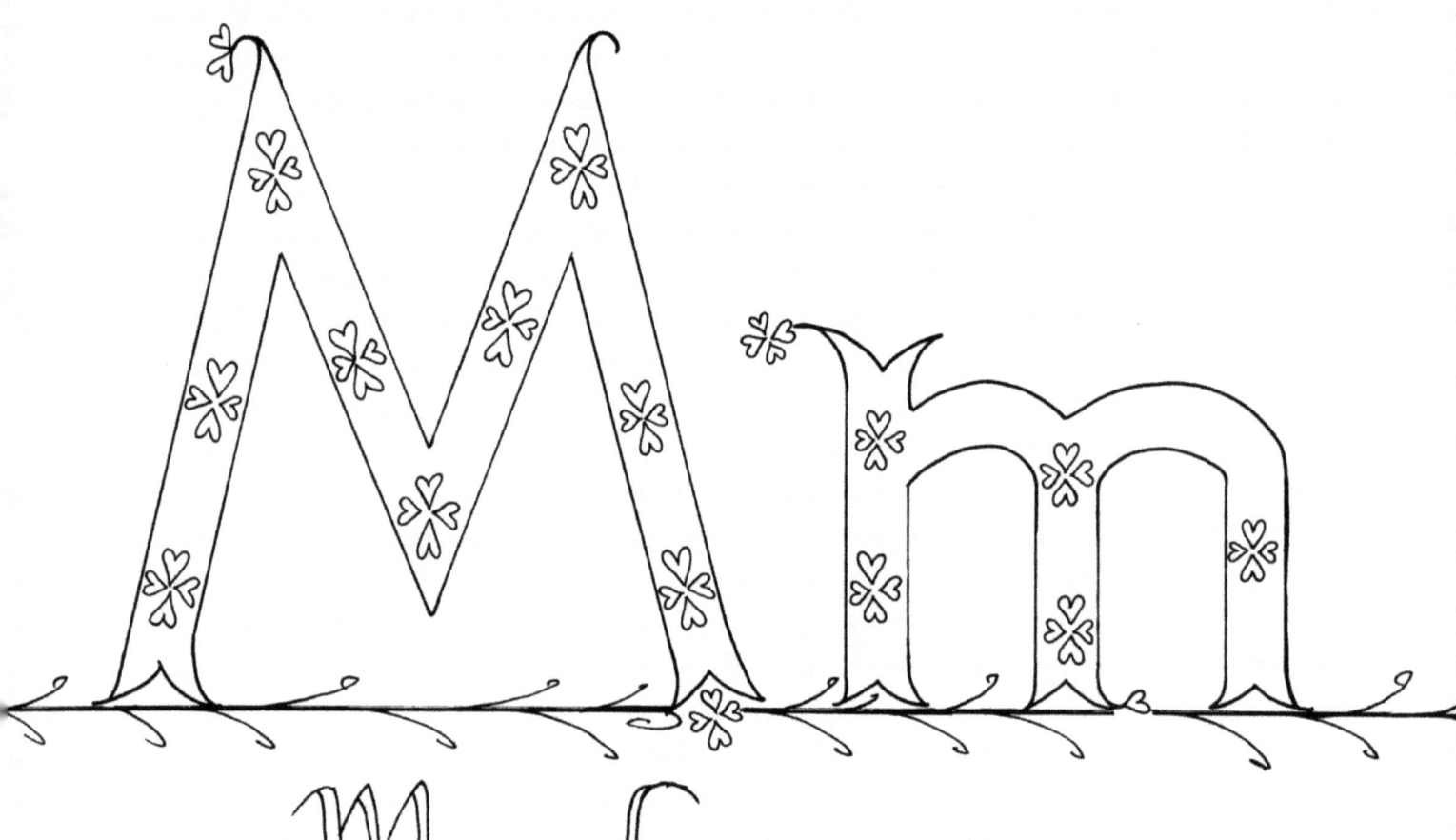

Mm
Mushroom
Sprung from intricately spun webs under the earth's musty veil

Quail

Headdress of tears
trembling in happy array.

Rose
Perfumed in soft pastels of petaled bliss

Snail

Sticky trails cannot hide where you have been

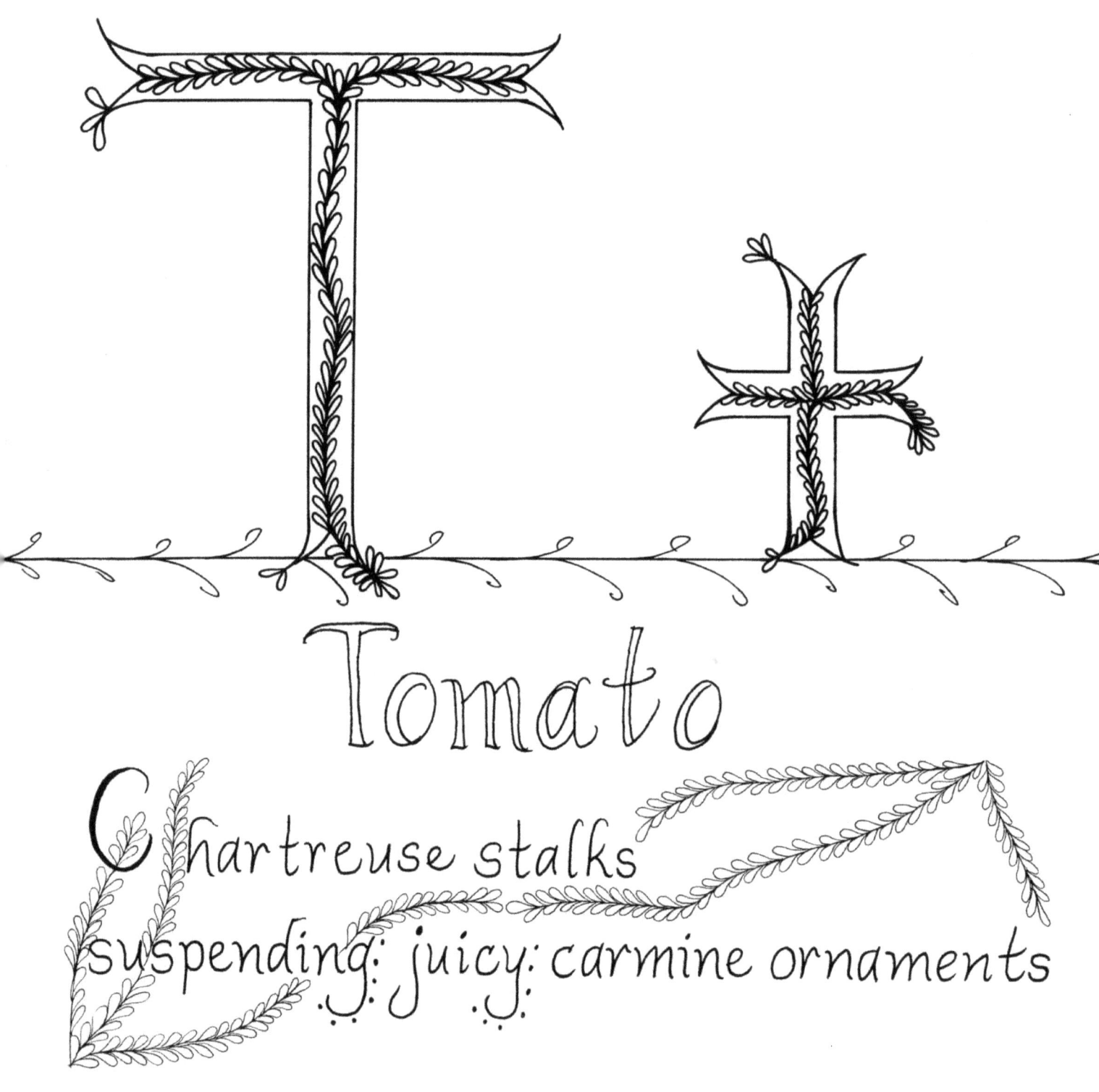

U u
Underwing Moth

Camouflage is the coat
that hides a heavily painted suit
of sweeping color

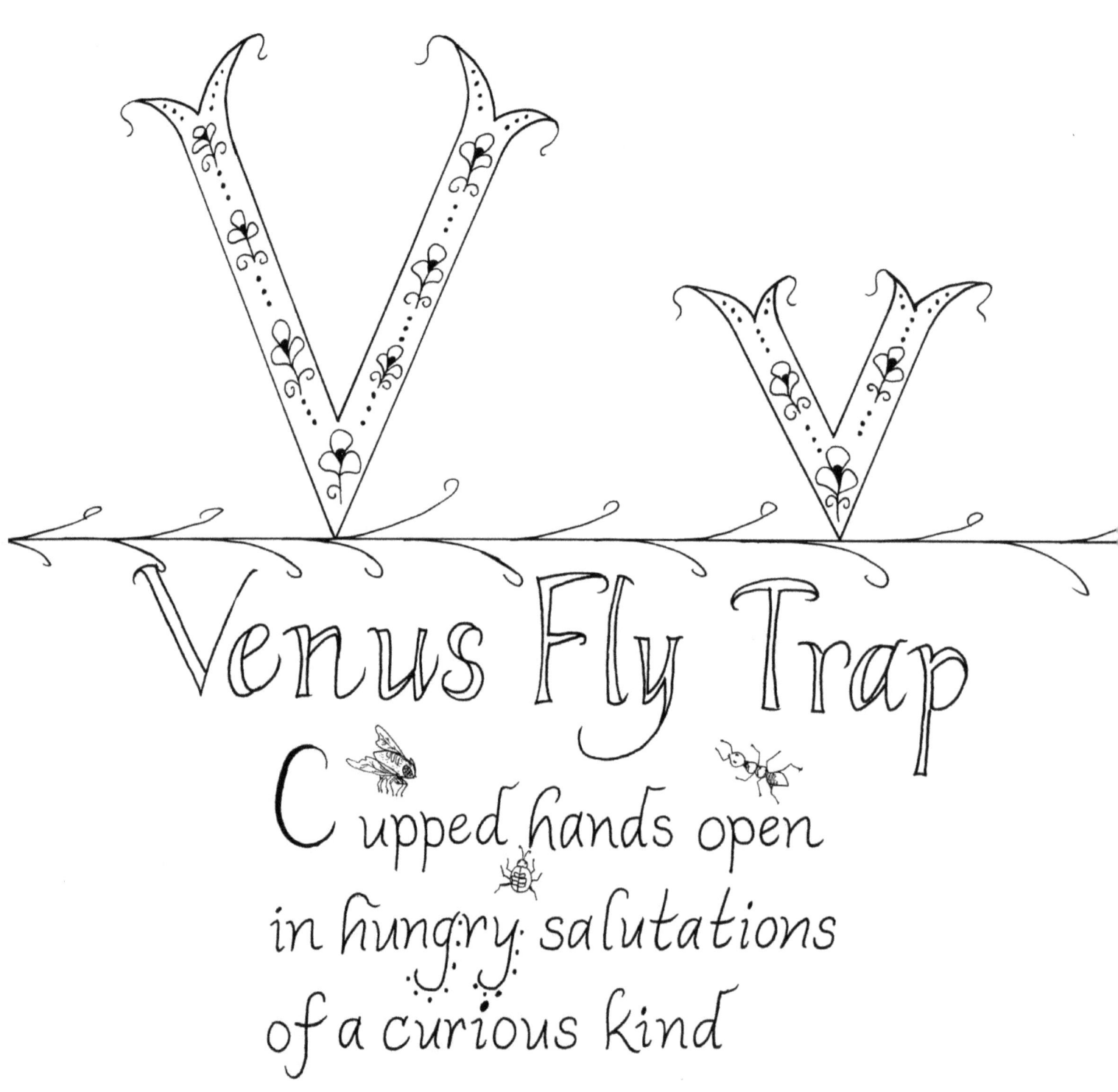

Venus Fly Trap

Cupped hands open
in hungry salutations
of a curious kind

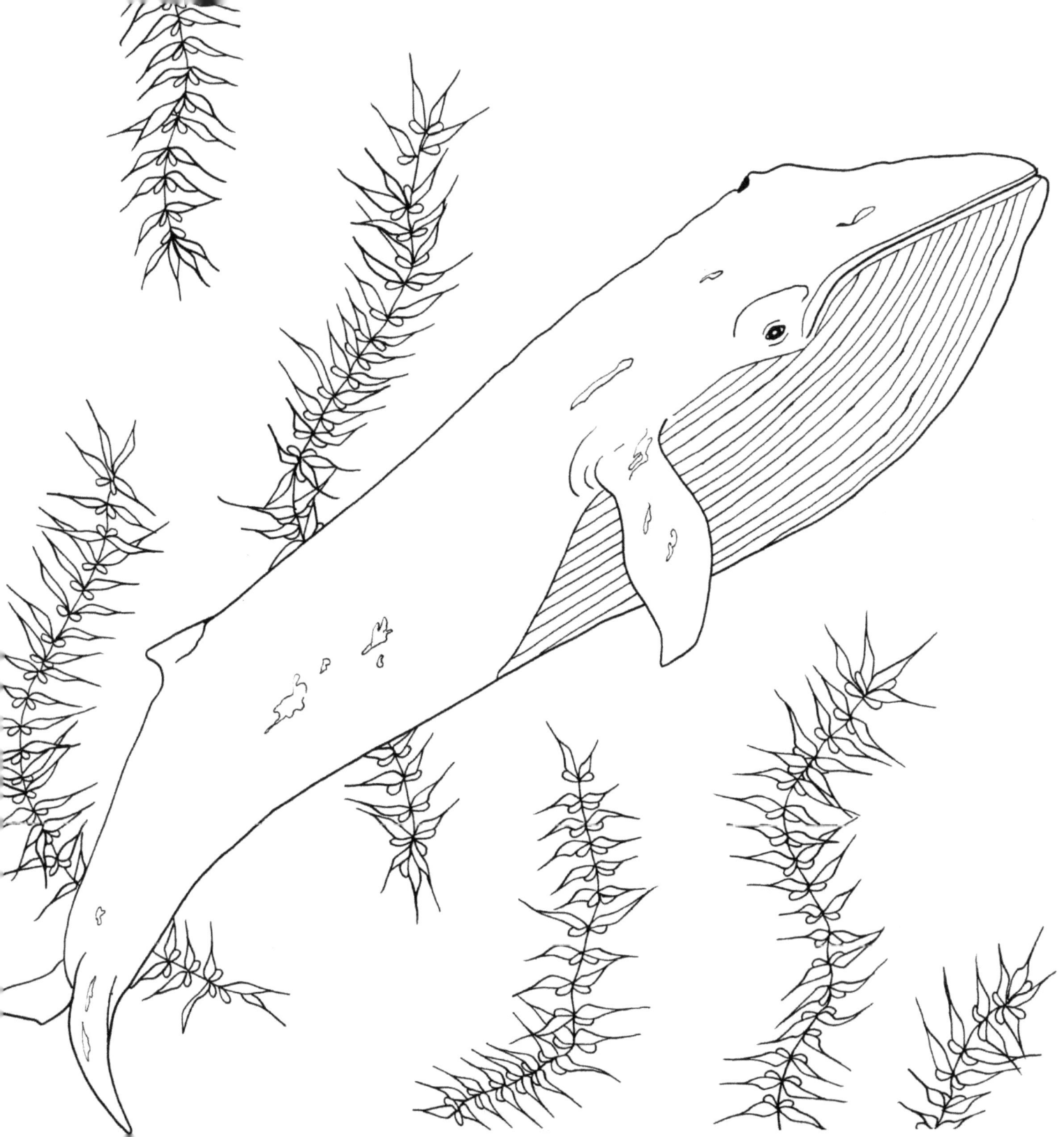

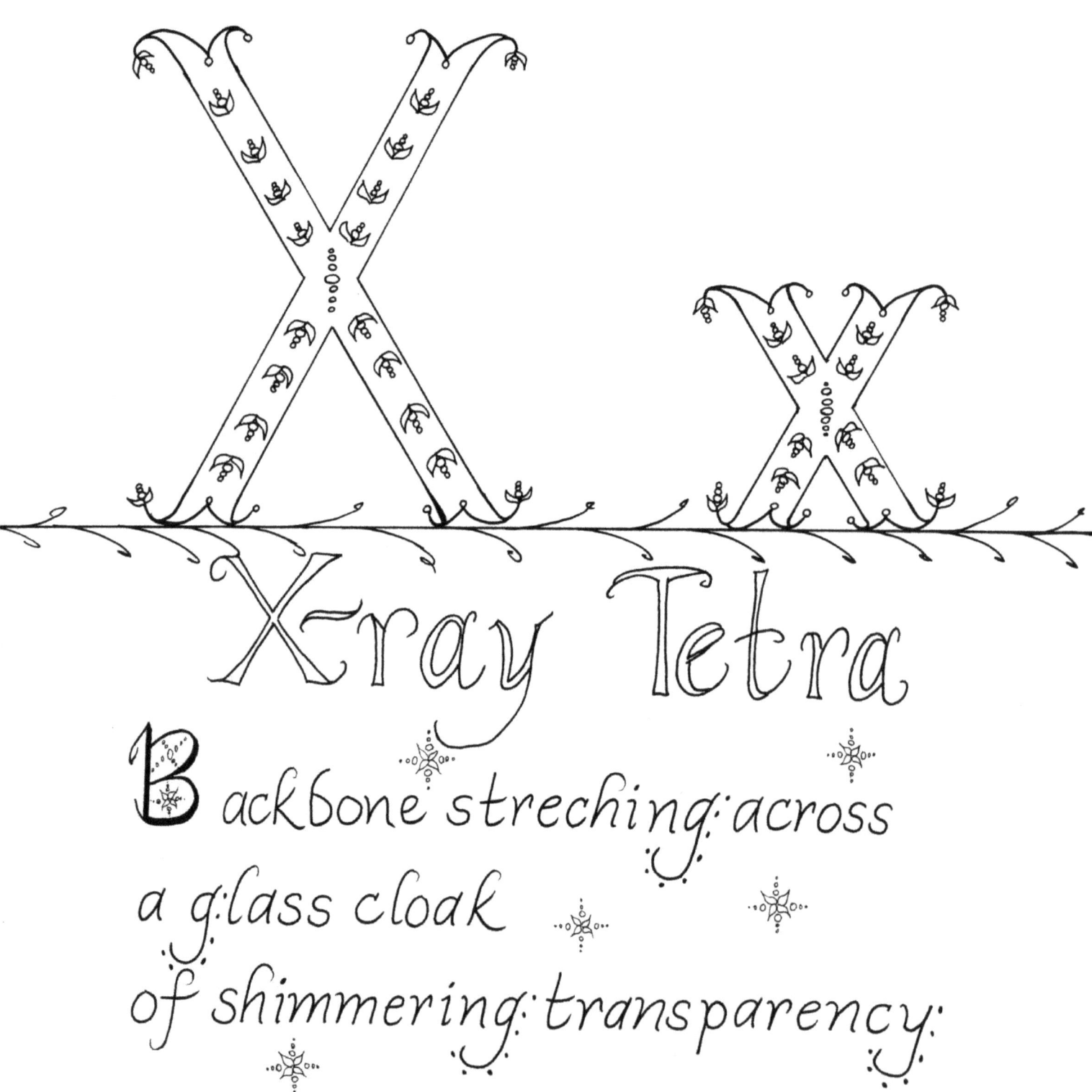

X-ray Tetra

Backbone streching across a glass cloak of shimmering transparency

Yy
Yellow Jacket

O happy needle hard at work
bulging out
of an ebony and gold stripped shirt

CPSIA information can be obtained
at www.ICGtesting.com
Printed in the USA
BVHW012024180523
664417BV00017B/261